The Country Life Picture Book of
Britain

The Country Life Picture Book of

Britain

Gordon Winter

Photography by
W. F. Davidson and R. Thomlinson

Country Life Books

frontispiece
The Langdales from Blea Tarn, Cumbria

Distributed for Country Life Books by
The Hamlyn Publishing Group Limited
London · New York · Sydney · Toronto
Astronaut House, Feltham, Middlesex, England

First published 1978
ISBN 0 600 31445 6

Printed in Spain by
Mateu Cromo Artes Gráficas S.A., Madrid

Introduction

Perhaps the most striking first impression to be gained from the following pages is how much of our visual heritage is still unspoiled. Nearly all the photographs were taken in 1976, and there is not likely to have been any great diminution in the standard of landscape between that time and the date of publication of this book. Nevertheless, the rate of change and destruction is still so great that one can only wonder whether the book will present an accurate record of the British landscape by the end of this century or whether it will be looked back on with historical interest as an impression of what our heritage was like before we allowed it to be destroyed.

In all Britain's wars in recent centuries, and particularly in the two World Wars, I believe that those who said to themselves that they were fighting for their country often meant country in both senses of the word: the nation, and the landscape. Certainly the matchless beauty of the English countryside was one of the ideals that the generation of Rupert Brooke and Wilfred Owen were fighting for. Matchless that beauty was and still is, though the splendour diminishes every year. What, then, are the qualities that give so unique and irreplaceable a character to the landscape of these islands?

It is often said that almost all our scenery is the product of the hand of man. The hills of Scotland were once largely clothed with the Scots pines of the Great Caledonian Forest. The bare or heather-covered hills that we now think of as characteristic were denuded of trees partly to provide timber for fuel and building, and partly because one of the ploys of clan warfare in past centuries was to go out and burn one's neighbour's forests. To those two influences must be added the clearances, which turned countryside inhabited by men into countryside inhabited by sheep, and later still the creation of artificially maintained grouse moors and deer forests.

South of the Border the hand of man was at work even longer and more energetically; cutting down the oak forests of the Weald to provide fuel for the iron industry; draining the fens; and invading and destroying the Greenwood all over England to provide more arable land for the needs of a growing population, and more grass for cattle and sheep.

Throughout British history men have been landscape architects, though it was only in the 18th century that the term began to be used self-consciously by those who so skilfully laid out the parks of great houses. Next to man, the other mammals that have had the most formative influence on our landscape have been sheep. In past centuries sheep, and especially their wool, played the part in the English economy that coal played in the 19th century, and that oil is beginning to play now. Not for nothing does the Lord Chancellor sit on a woolsack in the House of Lords. So it is not entirely accidental that sheep figure fairly frequently in the following pages. In this, however, I should declare an interest. Looking after sheep has long been among my part-time occupations, and for the past 20 years I have been shepherd to my own small flock. I did not guide the cameras of Mr Davidson and Mr Thomlinson, though I was more than happy to find that their predilection coincided with my own.

If the hand of man was largely responsible for giving Britain's landscape the qualities that we love and admire, what influence has been at work that has enabled that hand to produce results of such enduring merit? Why is the traditional pattern of an English village, of little houses grouped casually round church, squire's house and village green, so satisfying to man's emotional needs that whenever people can afford to do so they escape from industrial townscapes to live in the villages? What is it that has given the people of these islands their passionate and deep-seated love for the beauty of the countryside? Why have organisations like the National Trust and the National Trust for Scotland been conceived in Britain, to form a model for other countries to follow in the rest of the western world? Why do we still, for all the social and political follies of the past quarter-century, devote so much time and energy to town and country planning? Why are suburban gardens better kept in Britain than anywhere else in the world?

I believe that I know the answer to these related questions, though it would take a second lifetime of study before I could claim to be sure. I believe it is because English civilisation differs from that of France and Germany and Italy, and the other countries of Western Europe, in that it is not emotionally based on cities (as the word civilisation, the culture of cities, normally implies) but is emotionally based on the countryside.

In Italy, with scarcely a break since Roman times, most of the best things in life have centred on the towns, just as they did in the city-states of Ancient Greece. In Dante's day, as is made plain in the *Divina Commedia*, the city was the centre of solace, security and inspiration. The forests and mountains of the Italian landscape were dark and forbidding, and a traveller was glad to escape from them into the man-made beauty of the towns. Yet Chaucer, writing only a century later, looked outside the towns to find grace and life and inspiration in the countryside. And from Chaucer onwards it is the beauty of the English countryside that has remained the inspiration for the great bulk of our lyric poetry. I do not need, in these brief notes, to cite a long list of cases to support my argument. Anyone who doubts what I claim needs only to thumb through the pages of Palgrave's *Golden Treasury* or the *Oxford Book of English Verse*. Yet if one turns to French, German and Italian verse of the same periods, century by century, the emphasis on urban rather than rural pleasures continues. To cite a single further Italian example, this time in prose, the stories of the *Decameron* were told because Boccaccio's characters were so bored by the countryside, to which they had been banished by fear of the plague, that they had to tell each other stories to while away the time.

I am not saying that boredom in the countryside is never reflected in English literature (Jane Austen's young ladies were sometimes bored), but when it happens it is the exception rather than the rule. From the Middle Ages onward, English men and women of means had their hearts in their houses in the country; they came to town to transact business, to curry favour with the king, to gain the support of some great lord who was in London at the time, and later for a brief, fashionable 'season'. The letters of the Paston family, written to and from Norfolk in the 15th century, are the letters of men and women who, whenever they were in London, wished that they were back home in their good houses in the county.

It is from that background and tradition that the great houses of the English countryside sprang up. All over England, and to a lesser extent over Scotland, men who had enough money built themselves splendid homes, carefully sited in the landscape, and filled them, generation after generation, with fine furniture, pictures and books. Even today, in spite of almost a century of destructive taxation, the houses that adorn our countryside are among the wonders of the civilised world. The crowds that visit them, weekend after weekend in the season, are paying unconscious tribute to the principle that English civilisation, the culture of which they are a part, is rural rather than urban in its base. Through the centuries, Frenchmen have prospered in the countryside, making money out of the land, and have hastened to buy themselves homes in Paris as soon as they were rich enough to do so. Today, as in the past, the first thing that an emerging English family does, when it makes money in the towns though industry, commerce or the professions, is to buy itself a house in the country as a sign that it has arrived.

It is one thing to argue that English civilisation springs out of the countryside, and that the quality of our landscape and the quality of our civilisation have long been mutually supporting. By that I mean that the loveliness of the countryside has inspired our literature and music and painting, and the character of our civilisation has in its turn helped to mould and adorn the landscape. These points are not, I think, difficult to maintain. But why this should have happened in England, and to a lesser extent in Scotland, but not (or not to the same extent) in the related cultures of France, Germany and Italy is something that I find mystifying. Perhaps it is because we live in an island, and the whole island provides, in itself, the feeling of security and enclosure that continental peoples have only been able to create within the walls of cities. But that, though it may be true, can only be part of the story. Civilisations are not fertilised and cultivated merely by being enclosed, though the security that enclosure gives is one of their necessities. They are primarily caused to flourish by contact and competition between one man and another, one group and another, each striving to outdo his neighbour in the arts of war and peace. It is difficult to see why that kind of competition should have been stronger in the countryside in Britain than in the towns.

Perhaps the character of our culture is one of the results of the Norman Conquest, of the Normans' need to build castles all over the land, and to live in those castles rather than in the cities in order to hold down and dominate the strong-minded and obstinate people whose land they had taken. Perhaps if the English, the Anglo-Saxons, had been a servile and pliant people the Norman knights would have congregated in the cities once the Conquest was over, and the culture of the English counties would have become urban, like that of the princelings of Germany, and the Italian republics. Perhaps that is the heart of the matter: that the English great house is the direct cultural descendant of the Norman motte and bailey, and no further explanation is needed. Yet it seems to me that there must be some other cause. I do not know.

Once it is accepted that the flower of English civilisation springs out of the countryside and not out of the towns, then it follows inevitably that we must do everything in our power to preserve our countryside, to protect it from further urbanisation, and to avoid the destruction of our villages and country houses. Though village houses and small farmhouses often change use, and become commuters' homes, or second homes, at least they are preserved, which is a gain not to be belittled. For the past 30 years, however, we have allowed ourselves to indulge in a system of taxation that has made it harder and harder for the great houses, unquestionably among our principal national glories, to be maintained. This is an act of folly which succeeding generations will find it hard to forgive, whatever their beliefs and practices. If they believe in a system of liberty and private property, they will say that we should have amended our taxation to enable these houses, and their great collections of works of art of all kinds, to be maintained and lived in by the families who understood and loved them. If, on the other hand, succeeding generations in these islands believe in and practice communism, or any other kind of *étatisme*, then they will say that the State should have taken over this priceless heritage and kept it for generations to come. Either way, we shall be accused of criminal negligence for allowing the houses to come down and their contents to be dispersed.

The converse of my argument that civilisation in these islands is based on the countryside must be that our towns and cities are often surpassed by the urban civilisation of our West European neighbours. That point of view is not, I think, difficult to sustain. I doubt whether anyone would claim that we have cities in Britain that can match the perfection of Florence or Siena or Venice. Neither, I imagine, would anyone seriously claim that London, as a capital city, can be compared as a unity with Paris or Rome. Parts of London are of unrivalled beauty, but not the Great Wen as a whole. Edinburgh, of course,

stands out in splendour among British cities, and we can boast no other planned city like it. Oxford, Cambridge, Bath, all have their devotees, and I can hear angry voices raised in their defence; parts of these cities are breathtakingly beautiful – but not the cities as a whole. On the other hand, there are probably more individual buildings of outstanding quality in Britain, and more beautiful villages, than in any other comparably small area in the world.

What is the most beautiful single building in this country? That is a fascinating subject for argument, and can only remain a matter of individual taste. If I were asked to name one building that I should prefer to see left standing, if everything else were to be flattened or destroyed by a nuclear holocaust, I think I should pick the chapel of King's College, Cambridge (of which there is a fine and unfamiliar photograph on page 102). But it would be hard to leave out of the list Salisbury Cathedral, or St Paul's, or a baker's dozen of our great country houses. Everyone will have his or her list of preferences, and they will all be in a different order.

The point that I would make, however, in support of my general argument, is that in any such list of outstanding buildings the bulk would be found to be in the country, or in country towns. It is not by chance that the much painted and much photographed view of Salisbury Cathedral (seen on pages 106 and 107 in two contrasting views at different times of the year) shows the cathedral in a country rather than an urban setting. The great spire of Salisbury, majestic across the water-meadows and against an open sky, would lose its impressive serenity if it were hemmed in (and I do not doubt that some day either property developers or municipal planners will try to do just that to it). Yet the delicate needle of the Sainte Chapelle in Paris loses nothing by being half concealed, so that it is discovered as a sudden secret among the jumble of rooftops of the Palais de Justice. Salisbury is a rural concept; the Sainte Chapelle is essentially urban.

It will be a legitimate criticism of these pages that, though the book claims to be a picture book of Britain, it shows little or nothing of our industrial monuments, present or past. Partly this is because the 2,000 or so photographs from which I made this selection contained relatively few; but I doubt whether I would have chosen a higher proportion of industrial pictures, had I been able to do so. Industrial Britain, though it could provide splendid material for a collection of colour photographs, would perhaps be better treated as the subject for a book on its own. Within the compass of this selection, however, Abraham Darby's masterpiece (page 81), which has given its name to Ironbridge in Shropshire, is an admirable representative of the patterns that the Industrial Revolution has scrawled so exuberantly over the face of England. Abraham Darby's iron bridge of 1777 is by no means old if it is compared with, say, Stonehenge or the Roman Wall. In a thousand years' time there will, I would guess, still be evidence of the Roman Wall and of Stonehenge, because they were built of stone, and stone does not rust. I wonder how much of Darby's bridge will be left in the year 3000 AD, or indeed of many other monuments of the Industrial Revolution, simply because they were built of that highly perishable metal, iron.

Both Stonehenge and the Wall, however, are beginning to suffer from a new form of erosion which, within a short time, has done more damage than many centuries of battering by wind and weather. Unless we control the erosion caused by human feet and, at Stonehenge, by human hands as well, then even our most enduring monuments may not last more than another century or two. The time has already come when we have to say to visitors, at Stonehenge and similar vulnerable sites: you may stand and admire within, say, a distance of 50 yards, but you cannot come closer unless you are a bona-fide student of archaeology or are engaged in recognised research.

Even our mountains, which have been moulded for thousands of years by the erosion of sun and wind and rain, are beginning to crumble away because of the erosion caused by human feet. Snowdon is the worst victim so far, but it is not the only mountain to suffer. This is a major problem of landscape management, and we are still only fumbling our way towards a solution. In parts of the Lake District the National Trust has found that it can control human erosion by closing specific paths, or areas of mountainside, until they have had time to recover; but I suspect that that is no more than a temporary palliative in the face of the general problem of over-population, combined with increasing mobility and leisure. It seems to me inevitable that we shall have to devise some form of rationing of access, in some parts of the country, if we are to prevent crowds from destroying the scenery and the solitude that they have come to admire.

It may be noticed that many of these photographs depict the dramatic and therefore the untypical aspects of British scenery. They show less of the ordinary, everyday pattern of field and woodland, of which the greater part of the rural landscape is composed. Anyone who has pointed a camera will know, however, that one of the most difficult things to photograph successfully is the quality of ordinariness. It is the exceptional that tends to make photographs, just as it tends to make news. Mr Davidson and Mr Thomlinson have taken pains to record a fair proportion of everyday subjects; a good example of the ordinariness of farm landscape, which though commonplace is nevertheless the landscape that we most deeply cherish, will be found in the picture of a farm near Taunton, Somerset on pages 88 and 89.

Since the last Ice Age the British landscape has been continually changing, and most of the changes have, as I have said earlier in this Introduction, been wrought by the hand of man. Is there any point in complaining that man is continuing to change the

landscape in the 20th century? Undoubtedly the answer is yes. In the past, change has been gradual and organic; today it is so rapid, and the spread of urbanisation is so insidious, that unless they can be controlled the face of Britain may become unrecognisable within the next 50 years.

When the Town and Country Planning Acts were introduced, in the post-war years, it was hoped that they would put an end to the destruction of the countryside that had been going on in the 1920s and 1930s. To some extent the Acts succeeded, notably in the control of ribbon development and the exploitation of the landscape for private gain. The theory was that if the future of the landscape could be placed in the hands of the planners, all would be well. What has happened in practice, however, is that the planners have done nearly as much damage as they have prevented. New towns have been built on first-class agricultural land when, if they were to be built at all, they should obviously have been built on poor land. And the network of motorways, planned without any long-term consideration of the availability of petroleum fuels, has gobbled up fertile land as though we possessed an inexhaustible supply of it. Anyone who thinks that I am exaggerating need only consider the loss to agriculture caused by such horrors as the junction of M23 and M25 in Surrey.

In the past, of all the many influences that have fashioned our landscape, the most important has been the need to grow food. That need, the basic human necessity, is likely to prove the most reliable indicator when we are seeking guidelines to fashion the landscape of the future. Whatever else we may forecast about the future of these islands, it is clear that we shall need to grow more of our own food. We shall no longer be able to import half the temperate food we eat, as we have so heedlessly been able to do in the recent past.

With few exceptions, the landscape that is fashioned by efficient farmers will provide scenery that pleases the eye. I know that there are those who complain of factory farming, or of prairie farming when they see hedges being grubbed out to create larger fields. In some cases the destruction of hedges has gone too far, but when that happens it is not in the farmer's long-term interest and cannot therefore be described as efficient farming. Fields need to be big enough to be worked by today's machinery; we cannot hope to maintain the multiplicity of small fields that were enclosed when farms were worked by horses and oxen. Some hedges, and areas of woodland, must be retained because they provide shelter and windbreaks for livestock and crops, and because they provide a habitat for the wild life which is a part of the balance of nature, and without which efficient farming cannot continue. Almost all farmers now accept this.

It will be plain that I rate the protection of the countryside high in the list of national needs and duties. We may lose our liberties. We have lost many since 1945 and, as I write, it looks as though we shall lose many more before we again develop a form of central government strong enough to pursue coherent policies, to maintain law and order and to protect the weak against the strong. But it is not true to say that liberties once lost can never be regained. In British history we have lost and regained different aspects of freedom many times. The beauty and the fertility of the countryside are the basic elements of our heritage that we cannot afford to lose, or that we cannot afford to see further diminished. Together they are the source both of our spiritual and of our physical nourishment. If once we let them go they will be lost for ever.

* * *

All the 130 photographs in this book are the work of two men, W. F. Davidson and R. Thomlinson. Neither of them is a professional photographer in the ordinary meaning of that term. Mr Davidson is a clothier and mineralogist, but he is also a keen geologist, and that interest is reflected in his photography; he tends to photograph landscape, and particularly mountainous landscape, with an eye to the strata of which it is composed. Indeed, he photographs scenery much as a painter who has studied anatomy is able to paint the human body, with the bone and muscle showing plainly under the skin. He uses a Rolleiflex camera taking $2\frac{1}{4} \times 2\frac{1}{4}$ in. transparencies on Agfacolor film, and he works with a tripod when the need for depth of field lengthens the exposure. Mr Thomlinson is a retired local government officer. He uses Pentax cameras with 35 mm Kodachrome film, usually hand-held, and as far as possible he standardises on 250th of a second at about f4.5.

Both photographers are North-countrymen, living in Penrith and Carlisle respectively, and their preference for rugged scenery becomes apparent on a first inspection of their work. I suspect that they regard the gentle landscape of the South as a little soft for their taste.

When I first started looking through the 2,000 or so colour transparencies it became immediately apparent that the most difficult part of the work would lie in persuading myself to leave out pictures which were so good that they ought to have been left in. However, within the 130 photographs allowed I have tried to make a reasonably balanced selection, representative of the photographers' work and of the varied landscape of Great Britain. It will of course be plain that I had no initial say in what should be photographed. In general terms, however, I have been more than happy to accept Mr Davidson's and Mr Thomlinson's choice, though I might have wished to include more photographs of great houses, and particularly of great houses in the South of England, like Blenheim and Knowle, and I would have preferred to put views of Oxford and St Andrews alongside those of Cambridge. In making my own selection from the photographers' work I have never been tempted to omit views like those of the Seven Sisters in Sussex, or of Salisbury Cathedral across the Avon, simply because they were too familiar and much photographed; the criterion has always been that the pictures should show beautiful scenery beautifully presented.

There being no 'natural' order in which one can present an assembly of topographical pictures of this kind, I should perhaps explain, in case anyone is puzzled, that we have begun with Wales, gone on to Scotland and then gradually come down and across the map to London and the south-east. It will also be apparent in some cases that I have stuck to the traditional county names, or used both old and new. This has been done not out of conservatism, but because so many people still recognise the historic names and are puzzled by Avon, West Midland and other newcomers, and also because of the probability that many of the names and boundaries that date from the Local Government Act of 1972 may have been changed yet again before these pages have been long in print.

Gordon Winter.

Grazing in the Wye valley: sheep brought down from the hills near Llangurig, Powys (Montgomeryshire).

The Cader Idris range from Bwlch Oerddrws,
Gwynedd (Merioneth). The steep ridge of Cader
Idris – the chair of Idris, the warrior bard – runs up
to the summit of Pen y Gader at 2,927 ft. As Welsh
hills go, it is not particularly high, but it is one of the
most admired and visited, partly because it is easily
accessible from Dolgellau, some three miles to the
north, from which a choice of paths, varying in
difficulty, lead to the summit range.

Landscape architects at work: sheep grazing near Dolgellau, Gwynedd. The role of sheep in giving the hills of Britain their open, grass-covered slopes is nearly as important as the part played by man (see page 5). Without grazing, the slopes up to the tree-line would be covered – as they once were – by trees and scrub. As soon as stock are taken off for a number of years natural regeneration of forest-cover begins again, even where there is no deliberate re-afforestation.

The shepherd (*above*) on the slopes rising from
Tal-y-llyn continues his ancient craft undisturbed
by the railway, as his ancestors did before
it was built.

(*Right*) Tal-y-llyn, Powys. The name, which means
end of the lake, originally applied only to the village
on its shore, but has come to be used of the water
itself. When the Tal-y-llyn railway was built in the
middle of the 19th century, to provide transport for
the slate quarries, it was opposed (just as the Lake
District railway was passionately opposed by
Wordsworth) by those who sought to preserve the
peace of the valley. Yet by the middle of the 20th
century the railway itself had become a cherished
feature and was duly protected by a preservation
society. It is now a tourist attraction, and regular
passenger services are run, pulled by 19th-century
steam engines, throughout the summer.

(*Left*) Yr Wyddfa, in Gwynedd, or Snowdon, as it is generally known, is the highest mountain (3,560 ft) in England and Wales. Unfortunately, it is now so much visited that erosion by human feet is becoming a serious problem (see page 10).

(*Bottom left*) The skyline of Cader Idris from Bryncrug near Tywyn, Gwynedd (Merioneth).

(*Below*) Another view of Snowdon, here seen from Nant Cynnyd.

The river Wye at Rhayader in Powys (Radnorshire). Rhayader (the name means a waterfall) is a fishing centre as well as a market town, and though the average weight of trout is around $\frac{1}{2}$ lb the record weight is $10\frac{1}{2}$ lb, caught at Rhayader bridge. There are also salmon in the river, and in the past they were heavily and notoriously poached. This part of the Wye has changed little since it was described in the 1870s by Kilvert, the parson and diarist.

Farmed land near Llangurig, Powys. The river Wye, or Afon Gwy, is in its lower reaches here, and is about to join the Rheidol and reach the sea at Aberystwyth which, besides being a resort and university town, houses the National Library of Wales, celebrated for its collection of books in Welsh. The picture, together with the preceding views, is a reminder of the essential role of enclosed or in-bye land, without which hill farming cannot flourish.

Welsh black cattle above Llyn Clywedog. The lake is a man-made reservoir near Llanidloes in Powys.

The Snowdon hills from the Nant Gwynant, in Gwynedd. The river Glaslyn runs through this valley and through the little lakes of Gwynant and Dinas on its way to Beddgelert, some four miles downstream. In the upper reaches there are trout in the Gwynant, and sea-trout and salmon come up from Portmadoc, where the river joins the sea. At Beddgelert is the 'grave' of the legendary hound Gelert, who saved his master's child from a wolf and was killed by his master by mistake.

The llyn, or lake, of Gwynant. The nant, or valley, of
Gwynant, and the adjoining Nant-y-Gwryd, lie
among some of the finest mountain scenery in North
Wales. On the north-west side are Snowdon, the
Glyder Fawr (3,279 ft) and the Glyder Fach (3,262 ft).
To the east and south are Moel Siabod (2,860 ft)
and the two Moelwyn peaks (2,527 ft and 2,334 ft).
It is not often that Snowdonia can be seen in the
brilliant light in which the photographer was
able to take these two pictures.

(*Far left*) Harlech Castle overlooking Cardigan Bay. It must have been even more impressive in earlier centuries when the sea came right in across the levels, now marred by housing development. Built in the late 13th century, it is one of the finest Edwardian castles in Wales.

(*Left*) Portmadoc Harbour on Cardigan Bay. It lies some six miles north of Harlech beyond the levels seen opposite.

(*Below*) Caernarvon Castle, commanding the Menai Strait between Gwynedd and Anglesey. Another of the great Edwardian castles, built at the same time as Harlech but with polygonal towers in place of the more typical round towers.

Sunrise over the Strait of Scalpay, which divides Skye from the small Isle of Scalpay.

(*Below*) The stone circle of Callanish, Lewis, in the Outer Hebrides. This megalithic temple, one of the most important in Britain and generally ranked with Avebury and Stonehenge, is believed to date from about 1000 BC. The standing stones, of which the tallest is over 15 ft, form a circle round a chambered cairn. Their original purpose is unknown but is presumed to be connected with sun-worship; an avenue leading to the circle is aligned precisely north and south. How the great stones were transported and set up remains a mystery.

(*Right*) The white sands of Seilebost, near Borvemore on the south-west coast of Harris, Outer Hebrides.

(*Bottom right*) Plockrapool, on the south-east coast of Harris.

Loch Duich and the Five Sisters of Kintail,
Wester Ross. The sea–loch of Duich runs for some $5\frac{1}{2}$
miles south–east from the head of Loch Alsh. At its
landward end lies Glen Shiel below the Five Sisters,
of which the highest are Scour Ouran (3,505 ft) and
Sgurr na Ciste Duibhe (3,370 ft). The photograph
was taken in April with snow still lying on the higher
slopes. Much of the area is owned by the National
Trust for Scotland.

(*Below*) Ullapool and Loch Broom, Wester Ross. The photograph was taken from the road that runs north along the loch from the gorge of Corrieshalloch (National Trust for Scotland). Ullapool has flourished as a fishing harbour for two centuries, but as the herring fishing has declined the growth of tourism has helped to take its place. The street plan and some of the houses are attributed to Thomas Telford.

(*Bottom*) Loch Lurgain below Stac Polly (2,009 ft), Wester Ross.

Highland cattle at the side of Loch Quoich, Inverness-shire. The loch was inaccessible until the present road was built in connection with the Garry-Morriston hydro-electric scheme. Highland cattle, once the mainstay of Highland wealth, are still prized for their capacity to thrive in exceptionally tough conditions. They are now regarded as beef cattle but were originally a general-purpose breed. Their hardiness is carried on in the modern Luing cattle, a fixed cross between Shorthorns and Highlands.

(*Below*) South Obbe, Kyleakin, Isle of Skye.
Kyleakin lies on the Skye side of the ferry from the
mainland across the strait, or kyle, of Lochalsh.
Kyleakin's name is said to mean the strait of Haakon,
commemorating the Viking king who sailed through
the Kyle on his way to the battle of Largs.

(*Bottom*) The Cuillins of Skye seen across Loch
Scavaig from the hamlet of Elgol on the south
coast of Skye. The highest of the Cuillins is
Sgurr Alasdair (3,257 ft).

(*Left*) The Glenfinnan Monument at the head of
Loch Shiel, Inverness-shire. At the top of the tower
is a statue of a kilted Highlander, and on the walls of
the enclosure is an inscription in Gaelic, English and
Latin which tells the visitor that the monument,
erected in 1815, marks the spot where Prince Charles
Edward Stuart raised his standard on 19 August
1745. The monument is the property of the National
Trust for Scotland.

(*Below*) Early morning, Loch Laggan, Inverness-shire.

Sunset over the islands of Eigg and Rum from Arisaig, Inverness-shire.

Loch Eilt, Inverness-shire. Eilt is a small narrow loch with a name confusing even among Highland place names, in that it lies between Loch Eil to the east and Loch Ailort to the west. It is skirted by the road from Glenfinnan to the coast, and to the south of it are the hills of Moidart. The trees on the island are a reminder of what the Highlands looked like before the Scots pines of the Great Caledonian Forest were cut down (see page 5).

Loch Ailort, the sea-loch that runs out
into the Sound of Arisaig, west of Loch Eilt. The two
lochs, both skirted by the A830, occupy the same
narrow depression between Moidart and Morar,
separated only by a short stretch of low-lying land.
The small village of Lochailort, at the head of the
loch, is a good centre for enjoying the scenery of this
part of the Western Highlands, on the boundary of
Inverness-shire and Argyllshire.

The Royal Burgh of Culross, 12 miles west of the
Forth road bridge in Fife, is a remarkable surviving
example of Scottish domestic architecture of the 16th
and 17th centuries, when the little town flourished on
trade in coal and salt and a monopoly in the
manufacture of baking-girdles. Its present
appearance is the result of continuous restoration
over 40 years by the National Trust for Scotland.
The Trust owns a number of houses including the
Study (*left*) and the Palace (*below*).

Culzean Castle, Ayrshire, was built between 1772
and 1792 by Robert Adam. The Eisenhower Memorial
Rooms commemorate the President's tenancy
of a guest flat from 1945 to 1969. The castle was
given to the National Trust for Scotland by the 5th
Marquess Ailsa and the Kennedy family in 1945.

(*Below*) Pittenweem, Fife, one of several harbours
in the East Neuk where, as in Culross, restoration has
been carried out through the Little Houses
Restoration Fund of the National Trust for Scotland.

(*Bottom*) Beinn Alligin, the jewel mountain,
Torridon, Wester Ross. The three notched tops to the
right are the Rhans, or Horns, of Alligin. The centre
peak is Sgurr Mhor (3,232 ft) and the left-handed peak
is Meall an Laoigh (2,904 ft). They are on a 14,000 acre
estate owned by the National Trust for Scotland.

Loch Tummell, Perthshire. Though it is a natural loch, Tummell has been harnessed to provide power for hydro-electricity, with a dam at its eastern end, a short distance above Pitlochry. There is a sailing club at Foss, but Loch Tummell and Pitlochry, in the very heart of Scotland, provide a wide range of attractions for visitors, from ski-ing in the Grampians during the winter to pony-trekking and the annual Pitlochry festival in the summer.

Loch Lubnaig, Perthshire, lies along one of the two
most commonly used gateways to the Highlands: the
A84, which leads from Stirling through Callander
along the east side of the Loch to Lochearnhead; the
other is the Loch Lomond road, by Arrochar to
Inveraray in the south-west. The hills surrounding
Loch Lubnaig – Ben Vorlich (3,231 ft) to the north-
east and Ben Ledi (2,883 ft) to the south-west – give
many visitors to Scotland their first sight
of Highland scenery.

(*Left*) The Tweed as Sir Walter Scott saw it. Abbotsford in Roxburghshire was Scott's home from 1812 to 1832, and was conceived by him as a recollection of a number of historic buildings, including Linlithgow Palace. His descendants still own and cherish the house, with the novelist-poet's library and historical relics.

(*Below*) The Liddel Water at Penton Lynn near Canonbie, Dumfries-shire. The river forms the Border: Scotland on the right, England on the left.

(*Left*) The granary at Housesteads, Northumberland. Hadrian's Wall has survived centuries of neglect during which it was used as a quarry by anyone who wanted ready-cut stone. Now it, like Stonehenge, is suffering from too much attention (see page 10). The fort at Housesteads, one of 17 on the Wall, was given to the National Trust in 1930 by Professor G. M. Trevelyan.

(*Below*) Fountains Abbey, Yorkshire. In its great days the Cistercian monastery was one of the most splendid in Europe, with wealth founded on agriculture and especially on wool. At the Dissolution Henry VIII sold Fountains to Sir Richard Gresham. The extensive ruins are now publicly maintained.

(*Right*) York Minster, northern Europe's largest mediaeval cathedral, seen from the city walls.

(*Above*) Dry-stone walls near Malham, Yorkshire. When these walls were built, with much skill and labour, they were the most up-to-date and efficient way of enclosing fields. Now the fields are too small for modern machinery, and the walls are costly to maintain even if the skilled craftsmen are available. The walls are part of the Yorkshire landscape, and few of us would like them to disappear; but how is today's hard-pressed farmer to cope?

(*Left*) Autumn work with the sheep, Swaledale, Yorkshire. If the shepherd wants his ewes to lamb in March he will run the rams with them in October. So during that month he will bring his ewes in to make sure that they are in good condition and free of such troubles as footrot. At the same time he will raddle his rams, so that when a ram serves a ewe he leaves a tell-tale mark of coloured raddle on the ewe's hindquarters.

Lindisfarne Castle on Holy Island, off the Northumberland coast, reached by a causeway at low tide.

Seahouses, Northumberland, developed in
the 19th century as a fishing village but is now a
resort. It is a centre for boat trips to the Farne
Islands and for visits to Lindisfarne (see previous
page), both of which are properties of the National
Trust. Lindisfarne, built in the reign of Edward VI,
was restored by Lutyens in 1903. The Farne Islands
are a breeding ground for eiderduck, guillemot,
puffin, fulmar and other seabirds as well as for seals.

The Yorkshire coast, looking north-west
from Speeton towards Filey Brigg. Flamborough
Head is at about the same distance as Filey but to the
south-east. The photograph is a striking example of
the quietness of the many good beaches to be found
on the north-east coast of England. They remain
uncrowded and free of pollution, when there is
hardly room to move on many south-coast beaches,
partly because the south-east is more densely
populated but mainly because the Yorkshire coast is
generally not as warm. Nevertheless it is surprising
that empty beaches like this one can still be found at
the height of the summer season within a short drive
of Hull and York.

(*Left*) The Yorkshire Wolds, east of Malton. The chalk ridge in the East and North Ridings shares characteristics with similar chalk country in Lincolnshire and the Cotswolds – open land under grain and grass. But the 'wold', like the Weald of Kent and Sussex and the German *Wald*, is a reminder that these lands were once forests.

(*Above*) Carrying feed out to the sheep on Lune Moor, near Middleton in Teesdale, County Durham. The sheep-carrying capacity of a hill farm is limited to the number that the hills can feed in the winter, supplemented by what can be grown on the lowland fields or 'in-bye' land. Moreover in-lamb ewes, in the later weeks of pregnancy, are susceptible to twin-lamb disease, or pregnancy toxaemia, unless they are well fed.

Aysgarth Falls on the River Ure in Wensleydale, Yorkshire. The photograph shows the Lower Force, but the full extent of the falls, in a series of descending steps, runs for half a mile between cliffs of limestone, partly covered down to the water's edge with shrubs and trees. The Ure, one of the tributaries of the Ouse, is well known to anglers for its grayling, but it also offers trout and, in its lower reaches, coarse fishing.

Boulby Cliff, in the North Riding of Yorkshire. The cliffs are about halfway between Redcar and Whitby and are here seen from Staithes. The highest point of the cliff is 666 ft, which makes it the highest in England, though not in Britain, for it is dwarfed by many Scottish cliffs, notably Conachair (1,397 ft) and Boreray (1,245 ft) in St Kilda. It was from Staithes that James Cook, the explorer, apprenticed in a grocer's shop, ran away to sea, taking ship at Whitby.

The Pennine Way above Garrigill, Cumberland. The
walker who has travelled north along the Pennine
Way to this point will have left behind him Cross
Fell (2,930 ft), the highest point of the Pennines and
on the Way. On a clear day the view includes the hills
of Galloway and the Lake District. From Cross Fell
the path drops down to Garrigill in the valley of the
South Tyne and then goes north to Alston.

Dora's Field, Rydal, Westmorland (Cumbria).
Wordsworth lived at Rydal from 1817 until his death
in 1850. The one-and-a-half acres of Dora's Field,
once known as Rashfield, was bought by
Wordsworth in 1826 and planted with daffodils for
his daughter. His grandson, Gordon Wordsworth,
presented the field to the National Trust in 1935.
Wordsworth originally bought the land as a possible
site for a house, when he feared that he might have to
leave Rydal Mount.

(*Left*) Putting down hay for sheep after a snowfall below Saddleback, Cumbria. Sheep will graze in light snow by digging with their feet, but heavy snow presents the shepherd with an urgent problem, and long hours of hard work.

(*Bottom left*) Brotherswater and Kirkstone Pass, Cumbria, in winter.

(*Below*) The northern part of the Helvellyn range, Cumbria, from near High Bridgend.

The Penrith-Keswick gap, from Low Rigg, St Johns-in-the-Vale, Cumbria. The impression given by the photograph is of undisturbed tranquillity, but, in spite of protests, a dual-carriageway road now carries heavy traffic through the valley to Cockermouth and the west coast. It may be some consolation to think that in another hundred years, when the oil has run out, preservation societies will be formed to protect the motorways from disintegration, just as they now protect and restore 19th-century railways.

Borrowdale from the foot of Sty Head Pass, Cumbria. The view is looking north, down the dale towards Derwentwater, which is out of sight between the hills. The pass, fortunately crossed only by a footpath, connects Borrowdale with Wasdale to the south. Behind the photographer's back are Great Gable (2,949 ft), Scafell Pike (3,210 ft) and Sca Fell (3,162 ft). The whole area lies within the Lake District National Park. In addition many thousands of acres of the Lake District are owned by the National Trust.

(*Above*) Packhorse bridge across St John's Beck, St Johns-in-the-Vale, near Keswick, Cumbria. We are so accustomed to seeing stone arches incorporated in buildings, without any feeling of wonder, that it takes a simple example like this to bring back the sense of achievement such structures must have given to early masons and builders.

(*Left*) Gathering in for lambing, Mosedale, Cumbria. Mosedale is a recurring Lake District place-name. This one is south of Hesket Newmarket, between Caldbeck Fells and Bowscale Fell. The road is a minor one, and the tourist season has not yet begun, or the task of the shepherd, in driving down his in-lamb ewes without letting them become upset or anxious, would be harder than it looks in this peaceful photograph.

Yew Tree Farm, near Coniston, Cumbria: a unique shot of a much-photographed farmhouse.

Ashness Bridge, looking towards Derwentwater. The
countryside round Keswick is filled with records of
some of the greater names in English literature; turn
but a stone and start a poet. Among the ghosts who
might answer to a roll-call are Gray, Wordsworth,
Coleridge, Charles and Mary Lamb, Southey, Shelley,
Ruskin and Beatrix Potter. The magic persists
in spite of tourism, and other great names will
no doubt be added in years to come.

Derwentwater and Skiddaw from Shepherds Crag, Borrowdale. The photograph on page 69 shows the same stretch of country further up the valley. The photographer has now come some three miles down Borrowdale, so that the view has opened up and he has before him the island-dotted expanse of Derwentwater, backed by the snow-crowned summit of Skiddaw – known, wherever Macaulay's verse is read, as the last link in the chain of Armada beacons that 'roused the burghers of Carlisle'.

Compton Wynyates, Warwickshire. Pevsner, in his *Buildings of England*, describes Compton Wynyates as 'the perfect picture-book house of the Early Tudor decades'. Most of the house remains as it was built by Sir William Compton between 1480 and 1520, though it was originally defended by a moat. It was, of course, never intended to be a strong house in the sense that Bodiam (page 120), built only a hundred years earlier, was strong.

(*Below*) Middle Bean Farm, Stock and Bradley, Worcestershire. It is one of a group of three 16th-century houses, all timber-framed, though this one has brick chimneys.

(*Bottom*) Stone houses at Broadway, Worcestershire. Unwise though it is to nominate the most beautiful village in England, Broadway must have strong claims, because it displays so well the ability of builders over several centuries to design new houses without conflicting with their older neighbours.

(*Above*) Cottages at Wickhamford, near Evesham, Worcestershire. It is a reminder of the wealth of well-maintained cottages that survive in England that, though Pevsner discusses this village in the Worcestershire volume of *Buildings of England*, he refers only to the church and the manor-house, and the cottages do not rate a mention.

(*Left*) Early morning on the river Avon at Stratford. After the cumulative effect of three centuries of bardolatry, the remarkable thing about Stratford-on-Avon is that it has not been swallowed up in a morass of commercialism but has survived as a place of significance and beauty. Stratford-on-Avon, Ontario, has a setting so similar that this could almost be a photograph of either.

(*Left*) The packhorse bridge at Allerford, Somerset.

(*Bottom left*) Keble's Bridge, a clapper bridge over the river Leach, which connects Eastleach Martin with Eastleach Turville, in Gloucestershire.

(*Below*) The bridge of 1777, designed by Abraham Darby III, which has given its name to Ironbridge in Shropshire. The photographs on these two pages show three basic ways of solving the same problem. Abraham Darby's design was astonishingly advanced in its day. It was made possible because he had behind him the accumulated knowledge of his grandfather Abraham Darby I, who from 1710, at neighbouring Coalbrookdale, succeeded in smelting iron with coke instead of charcoal; and of his father, Abraham Darby II, who developed malleable iron from coke-made pig iron.

Wells Cathedral, Somerset, begun about 1186 and consecrated in 1239.

Combestone Tor, Dartmoor, Devon. Combestone hill is one of the steepest on the moor.

(*Below*) Widemouth Bay, near Bude, Cornwall. Bude Bay, of which this is a part, claims some of the best surfing beaches in England. At low tide the sea goes out for $1\frac{1}{2}$ miles.

(*Right*) Pentewan Sands, Mevagissey Bay, Cornwall. The whiteness of the sand is caused by china-clay washed down the St Austell River. China-clay, along with pilchards, smuggling and, more recently, tourism, has long been one of the principal sources of income on this part of the Cornish coast.

(*Bottom right*) Gunver Head, from Trevone Bay, near Padstow, Cornwall. Padstow was at one time on the pilgrim route from Ireland to Compostela in Spain, avoiding a sea passage round Land's End, and thus some of the worst dangers of Cornwall's rocky coast.

(*Below*) Glastonbury Abbey, Somerset. The ruins of
the Abbey and St Mary's Chapel, begun in the late
12th century, are Glastonbury's principal material
attractions; but legend claims that Joseph of
Arimathea buried the Holy Grail here, and that
King Arthur and Queen Guinevere were
buried in the Abbey.

(*Bottom*) Tintern Abbey, Gwent. One of the
most romantic ruins in Britain, Tintern was founded
by Cistercian monks in 1152.

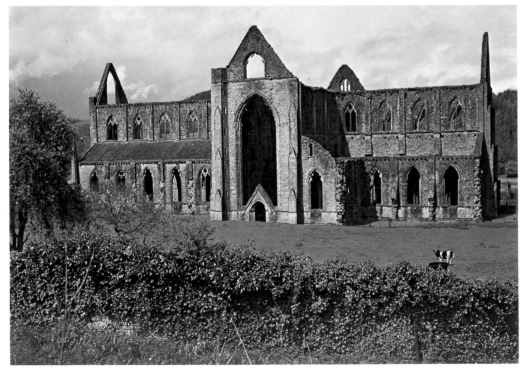

Berkeley Castle, Gloucestershire. The Castle
has remained in the hands of the Earls of Berkeley
since the Norman keep, still formidably strong, was
built in the reign of Henry II, 800 years ago. With its
exceptionally fine gardens, the castle has acquired
over the centuries an air of peace and serenity, but it
was here that Edward II was brutally murdered in
1327 at the behest of his Queen, Isabella, and the
Earl of Mortimer, after their successful rebellion had
dethroned him.

Near Taunton, Somerset: a landscape moulded by nature but worked by the hand of man.

(*Left*) Wayland's Smithy: a megalithic long barrow on the Berkshire Downs by the Ridgeway. A horse, left overnight with a suitable coin, would be shod by Wayland by the morning.

(*Bottom left*) Dragon Hill, Berkshire, where St George is reputed to have killed the dragon.

(*Below*) The Ridgeway, Berkshire: the best-known of Britain's prehistoric roads which follow the crest of a watershed.

The Grand Union Canal, near Bletchley, Buckinghamshire. As much a part of the fabric of England as the ancient trackways, the King's highways and the railways, the canals nevertheless enjoyed a comparatively short life. Their era began with the opening of the Bridgewater canal, Manchester, in 1761, and they were the main means of carrying the heavy products of the Industrial Revolution, notably coal and iron, until they were superseded, and often deliberately destroyed, by the railways in the mid 19th century. Their recent revival is partly due to their attraction for leisure craft.

(*Below*) Tile and thatch at Childrey, Berkshire. The healthy state of the craft of thatching in England is an encouraging reply to those who have forecast the end of the ancient village skills, except as artificial survivals. This is due partly to the practical advantages of thatch, and partly to the good work of the Council for Small Industries in Rural Areas, in training and encouraging apprentice thatchers.

(*Bottom*) The Fox and Hounds, Barley, Hertfordshire. Admirers of village pubs may reasonably claim that they are under-represented in this book; but here is a worthy example, in an aptly named village.

Great Chishill Post-mill, Cambridgeshire. This is a
good example of one of the earliest types of English
mill, in which the body of the mill, together with the
sails, is mounted on a central post so that it can be
turned to face the wind. Behind the mill is the fantail,
an invention added in the 18th century to the basic
pattern of the post-mill, which causes the mill to
turn into the wind automatically.

The Marsh-mill, Wicken Fen, Cambridgeshire. It is
a survivor of the many similar mills, at one time some
2,000, that made use of wind-power to drain the fens.
The National Trust first began to acquire land at
Wicken Fen in 1899, and the property has grown
with further gifts to over 700 acres. The nature
reserve is celebrated for its facilities for the study of
plants, insects and especially marshland birds,
for which it provides a breeding habitat and
migration refuge.

(*Left*) Castle Acre, Norfolk. An example of a planned, rectilinear village, in contrast to Childrey (page 93) which just grew. The castle from which this village is named is described by Pevsner as 'one of the grandest motte-and-bailey castles in England'.

(*Bottom left*) Cavendish, Suffolk. Another good example of the vigorous survival of thatch (see page 93) in one of the prettiest villages in the county.

(*Below*) Hilgay Fen, near Ten Mile Bank, Norfolk. The monks of Ely began reclaiming the fens in Saxon days, and the process has gone on slowly and unsteadily ever since; unsteadily because, though drainage produces new arable land of high quality, it changes a way of life and deprives marshmen of their traditional livelihood.

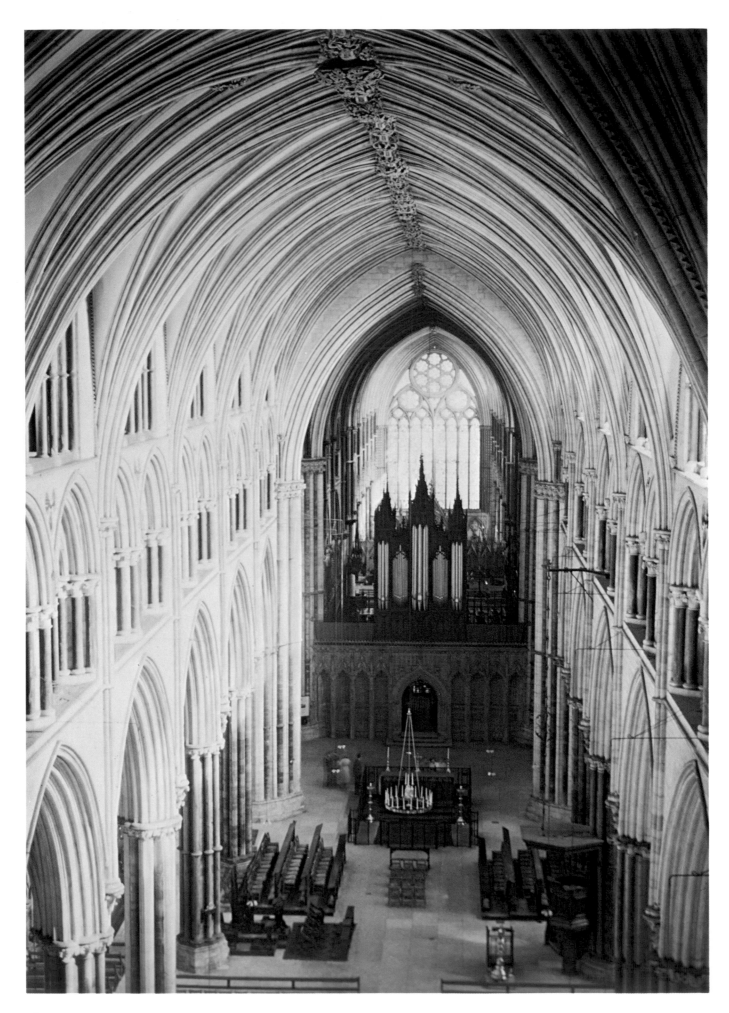

Lincoln Cathedral. (*Left*) The nave, vaulted about 1233. (*Below*) The partly Norman west front, with its three great doors. The cathedral, which owes much of its dramatic effect to its position on a hill dominating the city, is built in a succession of styles, but is in the main Early English. The 265 ft central tower, finished in 1311, was originally topped by a spire, as were the twin west towers, and houses the five-ton bell, Great Tom of Lincoln.

Norwich, like Lincoln, is dominated by its
cathedral, but less so because the cathedral is rivalled
by the great Norman keep of the castle. The
cathedral, consecrated in 1101, is mainly Norman
but with important later additions. The centre of the
city is still largely mediaeval and boasts 32 mediaeval
parish churches, a reminder that it once rivalled York
and Bristol in national importance. Its principal
source of wealth was hand-woven cloth, until the
Industrial Revolution outmoded it.

(*Below*) The church of St Mary, Dedham, Essex, built about 1500. Constable was educated at Dedham grammar school, and this church appears in many of his paintings.

(*Bottom*) Slack tide on the Blackwater estuary at Maldon, Essex. In spite of the boom in sailing, and Maldon's accessibility to London, the town has managed to preserve much of its mediaeval character. All Saints church has a 13th-century triangular tower, unique in England.

King's College chapel from Great St Mary's,
Cambridge. King's College was founded by Henry
VI in 1441, one year after Eton, from which school it
drew all its scholars until the 19th century. Work on
the chapel was begun in 1446, but it was not finished
until 1515. Its unusual shape – 300 ft by 80 ft by 40 ft
– achieves a sense of perfect proportion, and it is
widely considered to be the finest Gothic building in
England and perhaps in Europe (see page 8).

The Bridge of Sighs, St John's College, Cambridge. It was built in 1831, to join the College's New Court with older buildings on the other side of the Cam. It takes its name from the 16th-century bridge in Venice across which condemned prisoners walked to prison. The horizontal iron bars across the five unglazed windows were put in to prevent undergraduates from using the bridge as an easy way of climbing into the college after the gates were shut at night.

Spring in the New Forest, near Minstead, Hampshire. The forest was created, largely on settled land, from 1079 by William the Conqueror, who decreed that a 'mickle deer-frith' be made to provide him and his court with hunting. It is doubtful whether any action by the Normans caused wider or more bitter resentment; yet it is a celebrated reminder of the continuity of English habits that we still call it the New Forest. The Forest extends over some 90,000 acres and presents in many areas an unchanged mediaeval aspect, including the sight of pigs running loose to feed on the mast from the beech trees. New Forest ponies, one of our nine native breeds, are much valued for their good temperament.

The changing seasons at Salisbury, Wiltshire. The cathedral, much painted by Constable and others, photographed (*below*) in late April and (*bottom right*) in early September (see page 8). Salisbury's spire is a 14th-century addition to an otherwise Early English unity, the whole cathedral having been built within a space of 60 years. There is no earlier work because the see moved from Old Sarum in the 13th century and Salisbury was built, complete with cathedral, as a new town.

(*Below*) Castle Combe, Wiltshire, has suffered from having been thought the most picturesque village in England, and has attracted too many visitors for its own comfort. It has, however, survived, due to local care and determination; and even Pevsner, not given to excessive praise, admits that it is unspoiled 'except by over-restoration and tidying-up of the houses'. Celebrated features are the late 17th-century dower house, the market cross and the 17th-century manor house.

(*Below left*) Bosham harbour, Sussex. Bosham is thought of mainly as a holiday town, much admired by today's ever-growing band of sailing enthusiasts, but its roots could hardly lie deeper in English history; in 1064 King Harold sailed from Bosham, was shipwrecked, fell into the hands of William the Bastard, and swore (or so it was claimed) an oath of fealty that led to Hastings and the Norman Conquest.

(*Below right*) The Chesil Bank, Dorset. This pebble beach, unique in Britain, runs for some 18 miles north-west from Portland to Abbotsbury. The pebbles get steadily smaller all the way from south-east to north-west.

(*Right*) Portland limestone on the Dorset coast, looking east from Stair Hole.

(*Below*) Lacock Abbey, Wiltshire. Once a nunnery, and from the 16th century a country house, Lacock was the home of W. H. Fox Talbot, inventor of negative–positive photography. The second oriel from the right was the subject of his first negative, made in 1835.

(*Bottom*) High Street, Lacock. Lacock Abbey and most of the village were given to the National Trust by Miss Matilda Talbot in 1944.

The great stone circle at Avebury, Wiltshire.
Larger and more impressive than Stonehenge, it
remains less known.

(*Below*) The Albert Memorial, Kensington Gardens, London, built between 1863 and 1872.

(*Right*) St James's Palace. Most of the palace dates from Henry VIII, but Wren and Hawksmoor are among architects who have made later additions.

(*Bottom right*) Daffodils in St James's Park, London. The photograph shows no tall buildings, but already they are beginning to overshadow and shrink the park.

Buckingham Palace and the Victoria
Memorial. In Services slang, the palace is still 'Buck
House', a reminder that the Sovereign's principal
residence was built as the Duke of Buckingham's
country house, just outside London, in 1705. Most of
the present palace dates from the 1830s, much of it
by Nash, and the familiar east front, seen here, is as
recent as 1913. As Pevsner has pointed out, it is
part of the Englishness of the palace that Nash
kept it a country house.

(*Below*) Hampton Court Palace, presented to Henry VIII by Cardinal Wolsey in 1529, remained a royal residence until the reign of George III. William III commissioned Wren to rebuild the palace and demolish the Tudor courts, but died before the demolition was carried out.

(*Bottom*) Whitehall, looking north. On the left are the Treasury, the old Home Office and the Foreign and Commonwealth Office. Beyond Lutyens' austere Cenotaph is the old War Office.

The Tower of London: fortress, palace, prison, barracks and zoo have been some of its many roles.

(*Left*) Mermaid Street, Rye, Sussex.
(See also page 124.)

(*Bottom left*) A corner of the churchyard,
Winchelsea, Sussex. Winchelsea, one of the Cinque
ports, was a New Town in the late 13th century,
when Edward I ordered it to be built to replace a
lower-lying town overwhelmed by the sea. England
has been secure from full-scale invasion for so long
that it is often forgotten that in the 14th and 15th
centuries Winchelsea was repeatedly attacked and
sacked by French raiders.

(*Below*) Weatherboarded and tile-hung houses at
Cranbrook, Kent. The row is typical of the well-
proportioned and well-preserved small houses in this
pretty Wealden town, which also boasts a fine
church, a celebrated 16th-century school and a
smock-mill.

Bodiam Castle, Sussex. Bodiam was built in
1385 as a response to the sacking of Winchelsea and
Rye by the French. The present state of the castle is
largely due to the vision of Lord Curzon, who bought
Bodiam in 1917, devoted much energy to research
and restoration, and left the castle to the National
Trust in his will. It stands now as a symbol of
the last age of castle building and as a memorial
to a great Englishman.

(*Below*) The South Downs near Alfriston, Sussex. Robert Bridges wrote of them as the 'bold majestic downs, smooth, fair and lonely' and it is to the credit of our post-1945 planning laws that they have to a large extent retained those qualities, in spite of their accessibility from the south-coast resorts and from London.

(*Bottom*) The Long Man of Wilmington, Windover Hill, Sussex. The best known and loved of England's prehistoric chalk-hill figures, he stands 226ft high.

Where the South Downs meet the sea: the Seven
Sisters, Sussex. These rounded chalk cliffs run
westward from Birling Gap to Cuckmere Haven and
have been formed by the sea's slicing off the ends of
seven parallel chalk ridges. Some 700 acres of the
cliffs, with the downs and valleys behind them, have
been acquired by the National Trust since 1928.
Along them runs a footpath which is part of the
80-mile South Downs Way.

Marsh behind Winchelsea beach, Sussex. Marshland like this is one of Britain's diminishing assets, but where the marshes survive they provide a vital breeding habitat for water birds such as reed- and sedge-warblers, shovelers and water-rails, and a nesting place in spring and autumn for such migrants as common terns, garganey and a variety of waders. In past centuries, before they were reclaimed, wide areas of neighbouring Romney Marsh and Walland Marsh must have looked like this.

(*Left*) The Mermaid Inn, Rye, Sussex, built mainly in the 15th century and little changed. Rye, an ancient Cinque port like its neighbour Winchelsea, suffered equally from French raids in the 14th and 15th centuries.

(*Bottom left*) Sheep on Walland Marsh, near Camber, Sussex.

(*Below*) The Cuckmere River winding between the South Downs near Alfriston, Sussex.

Near Worthing, Sussex: west wind and driving rain
provide an appropriate tailpiece to this pictorial
record of Britain's landscape.

Acknowledgments

The photographers were responsible for the illustrations as
follows:

W. F. Davidson: frontispiece and pages 11, 14–15, 16, 17,
18–19, 21, 22, 23, 24–25, 26, 27, 28, 29 (both), 30–31, 34–35, 35
(both), 39, 40–41, 42–43, 43, 44, 45, 46–47, 47 (both), 48, 49, 50,
51, 52 (both), 54–55, 55, 59, 60–61, 62, 63, 64, 65, 66 (both), 67,
68, 69, 70–71, 71, 72–73, 74, 75, 76–77, 77 (both), 78–79, 79, 80
(both), 81, 84, 85 (both), 86 (both), 86–87, 88–89, 90 (both), 91,
92–93, 93 (top), 94, 95, 96 (bottom), 101 (both), 103, 104–105,
106–107, 109, 110 (both), 110–111, 112, 113 (both), 114–115,
115 (both), 118 (both), 119, 121 (both), 122, 123, 124 (top), 125,
126–127

R. Thomlinson: pages 8–9, 20 (both), 32, 33 (both), 36–37, 37
(both), 38, 53, 56–57, 58–59, 82, 83, 93 (bottom), 96 (top), 97,
98, 99, 100–101, 102, 104, 107 (both), 108 (both), 116–117,
120–121, 124 (bottom)